SUNSHINE, RAIN

Love and Pain

SUNSHINE, RAIN

Love and Pain

PAULA DUGGINS

Sunshine, Rain: Love and Pain

Copyright © 2018 by Paula Duggins

Dedication

First,

I give honor to God for the gifts He has given me to be used to His glory. Thank you Father for your patience as you have waited for your daughter to be obedient.

Secondly,

I dedicate this book of love to my five beautiful children
Joy, Tony, Angel, Jasmine, & Cameron who are the greatest and most precious gifts of love I have ever received. And to my daughter to whom I did not give birth Carlina.
You all are my Sunshine.

Lastly, but definitely not least,

I dedicate this book to the special man in my life, affectionately called "Reevey"
with whom I have shared both the joys and pains of Sunshine and Rain

TABLE OF CONTENTS

I SUNSHINE

II Intermission: Love Duets

III Rain

ACKNOWLEDGEMENTS

I would like to thank the late Elbert "Sonnie" Duggins for his everlasting love, for always believing in me and speaking positive and encouraging words over me in my youth. Daddy, this is only the beginning; there is more to come and I love you eternally.

I thank my mother Lou Bland for her love and guidance throughout my entire life.

To my sissy "Tracy Duggins" for being my cheerleader almost all my life and always encouraging me.

I also want to thank my young cousin/fellow poet/sounding board & listening ear, Raven Bland, for all the countless days and late nights of sharing poetry, songs, and rhymes in our self-proclaimed "no judgment zones". It has been wonderful enjoying this poetic journey with you.

FOREWORD

"Some poets have to paint a vivid picture through similes and metaphors, or even personal stories to make the reader understand their emotions. The way Paula's words bounce up and down on the page and roll you to the last period, Paula's writing doesn't need a plethora of metaphors, nor a picture; she massages the reader into FEELING what needs to be understood. That's the magic of Paula's writing: her powerful simplicity will have you singing her words around the house, bopping to her rhythm and blues while driving to work, and ringing in your ears in between. Sit back, clear your minds and your calendars, and I hope you get to feel the love I get to experience all day and every day from Paula Duggins."

Raven Bland,
Norfolk 1st Youth Poet Laureate,
Author, "*When The Raven Sings...*"

PREFACE

Sunshine & Rain was birthed in my heart many, many years ago, when just like the average young lady of youth, I was on a quest to find love. I was, as my sister Tracy says it best, "in love with being in love". We laughed and joked about this often, but as I matured I found it not only to be true, but also to be okay. Yes, I said it, it is okay to have loved and lost and to have endured the misadventures that come along with being vulnerable. I didn't mind being laughed at for wanting to give love and to be loved in return. For after all, the greatest book of all times, the Bible, speaks of love quite frequently and yes even of a romantic love. For in Song of Solomon 3:4 Solomon proclaimed "I have found the one whom my soul loves." So it is indeed human nature to desire love. Yet, love runs much deeper than everything being lovely at all times. It takes great maturity to understand, withstand, and appreciate that life requires both sunshine and rain and that the two simultaneously complement one another. In my opinion, the joy of loving outweighs the occasional pain, and just like the earth needs the sun to shine, it also needs the rain to grow. Love with no pain is unrealistic and I prefer to have lots of love with some pain along the way then to never have loved at all.

Introduction

Love

"Bears all things, believes all things, hopes all things, endures all things"

1 Corinthians 13:7

This book of poetry expresses the highs and the lows of love and invites you to embrace the joys and the pain, and consequently the Sunshine and the Rain.

I

SUNSHINE

GOOD MORNING SUNRISE

Good Morning Sunrise

I love the Beauty in your eyes

And your strength that makes me rise.

Your warmth makes me tingle between my thighs

Reminding me I am still alive.

Again, I say good morning Sunrise.

It is no surprise

That it is indeed you I see when I open my eyes.

Your warm rays are a wonderful welcome to a new day.

Shine my love, shine,

You are a reminder that yesterday is left behind.

I am blessed that you shine my way.

Good morning Sunrise

Have a great day

Muuuuuuuuuaaaaahh!!

SUNSHINE

The sun boldly and brilliantly emerges from behind the clouds.

Its rays radiate my entire being, and saturate my soul

Allowing me to leave all my worries and cares behind

Its radiance hypnotizes my mind

And sends me on a journey that covers a span of time

That contains my past, present, and my future

I watch as it paints its own self-portrait

Splattering hues of color in the most unimaginable places

Creating a scenery that captures and accentuates its inner and outer beauty

Your Smile

S   Your smile is the **sunlight** that brightens my life throughout the day

M   Your smile is the **moonlight** that leads my path by night

I   Your smile **illuminates** everything within me that no one else can see

L   Your smile reveals true **love** and hidden **laughter**

E   Your smile adds **exuberance** and **excitement** to my entire life

SEASONS

To everything there is a time and a season:

The Spring-is a time of new life; animals give birth, seeds sprout, flowers bloom; most animals, sprouts & flowers survive, yet some do not. Those that do survive, give a vibrant, refreshing, exhilarating, and exciting fragrance to the earth around it.

The Summer- those things that were born continue to grow and flourish;
a time of warmth, enjoyment and relaxation; those things that survived
are strengthened by the summer heat.

The Fall- Things begin to shed or fall off and therefore never make it to the winter; a time of new harvest; a time to gather and to give thanks for what remains.

The Winter- Those things that remained during the Fall are left to survive the winter; a time of cold and harshness,
yet refreshing, because the winter cold kills off the germs and prepares things for the upcoming spring.

If things survive the winter, they have proven their
strength and steadfastness and therefore are welcomed
once again into the spring.

It has been said that people come into your life for a
season and a reason;
Whatever the season and whatever the reason,

and for however long it lasts,
I am glad that you came into my life.

TWENTY YEARS LATER

I can't believe it has been twenty years
Since the day you left my side
and my true feelings I decided to hide.
We said our goodbyes and we shielded our cries.
We both decided to move on with our separate lives.
Twenty years is such a long time
To leave your real true love behind.
As time moved on
So many people have come and gone.
Yet, we both still seem to be so alone.
Thinking of each other often
and remembering the great times we had,
Wondering where the other was and
Not knowing, made us both very sad.
Twenty years later,
here we are;
Realizing that the distance between us
Wasn't really that far

And that our true love that once was intercepted,
Has been waiting quietly to be reconnected.
Twenty years later, our love is still very strong
And to this wonderful relationship
we better hold on.

WHY DO I NEED THEE

Why do I need thee?

Let me count the reasons…

One, I need thee because you are a fulfillment of all my seasons;

Spring, Summer, Winter, & Fall,

You are a resemblance of them all.

Two, I need thee to help fill all my nights and days.

Three, I need thee because I love your soft and gentle ways.

Four, I need thee because you are my sunrise and my sunset.

Five, I need thee because you are the sweetest most loving man I've ever met.

Six, I need thee because you were made just for me.

Seven, I need thee because the real me, only you can see.

Eight, I need thee because with you, I am free to be me.

Nine, I need thee because we fit together like a hand in a glove

Ten, I need thee because you are the one man that

I truly love

WHEN WE ARE TOGETHER

When we are together, people see you and they ooh and

aah over your size, height, and statue because you are

so tall and your shoulders are so broad and wide.

But me, as I walk by your side,

I see what they cannot see…

The even greater statue of the inner you that is

submerged deep inside.

I look up at you and into your beautiful brown eyes

And I can see deep down into your warm soul.

I see a strong man with sweet and gentle ways

Who just wants to love and be loved in return.

As I hold your hand, I feel your warmth radiating

from your heart to mine,

And I feel so safe and secure with a man

who loves so unconditionally and gives so willingly.

LOVE YOU, STILL

I love you still,

Always have,

Always will.

I loved you from the start,

I've always had you in my heart

Even when we had to part.

I love you still,

Always have,

Always will......

TODAY

Today, I awakened to thoughts of you and I'm still mesmerized

because I realize the dream is actually true.

Today, I visualized you as you lay across my bed and upon

your strong broad chest I lay my head.

Today, I reflect upon your sweet and tender kiss and

I think about the fact that I've never loved like this.

Today,

I reminisce

As it is you that I truly miss

CONSUMED

I am consumed with meditations of how our past

has merged into our present and is transforming our
future.

My thoughts are engulfed in the flames of passion

That are blazing rapidly out of control.

My heart is overwhelmingly flooded with a multitude

Of emotional precipitations that are saturating

The chambers of my heart almost to the point of
suffocation;

Breathing is sporadic and my pulse is rapid.

I'VE LEARNED

I've learned

That when you find something special

That you know is a rare treasure,

That you don't wait to possess it

When you think the time is right;

You need to seize it that very moment

And hold on so very tight.

For if you wait…

Miss out on a good thing,

You just might;

Therefore,

I plan to hold on tight!!

What's Going On

I'm trying to figure
What is going on;
You got me singing all these love songs
I'm talking
A
ALLLLLLLLL day long..

Then when I get home
I just don't want to be alone
And I have to call you on the phone
To hear your voice and talk
ALLLLLLLL night long..

I'm talking from
dusk till dawn.
What is going on?

Whatever it is,
keep it going strong,
I want to keep singing these love songs.

LOOKING AT YOU LIKE THAT

You once asked me why I am looking at you like that,
Well this is my reply…
And I hope you are ready for the answer
Because the eyes do not lie.

I am looking at you like that
Because it is through the eyes
That our two hearts first met.

I am looking at you like that
Because it is through our eyes that we connect.
My soul is speaking to your soul
In a language that only they can understand,
So that is why I am looking at you like that, my dear man.

I am looking at you like that
Because when our eyes meet
They record the rhythm
of our every heart beat.

I am looking at you like that
Because I am mesmerized
By what I see way beyond your eyes.

I am looking at you like that
Because my eyes are the voices of my heart,
And they speak the truth of its every beat.
For the rhythm of my heartbeat is a language
That only the eyes can decipher.

I am looking at you like that
Because your positive energy
Radiates from the iris of your eyes
To the center of my thighs,
And remind me that I am still alive

I am looking at you like that
Because you amaze me,
And you please me in many ways
that only the eyes can see.

I am looking at you like that
Because I see in you
Everything that completes me
And it is through your eyes
That your soul greets me.

SUNSHINE 2

Like the sunshine brightens a day

You make me feel everything is okay.

Since you came back into my life

You re-entered my universe with your illuminating smile.

You are my Sunrise and my Sunset

Your love I can never forget.

THEY SAY LOVE IS BLIND

They say love is blind but I disagree
For there is much that love can truly see

Like the shadows of you and me
Sharing each other so secretly

Or the way you look at me
As though I am the only person that could ever be
Or the way you hold and caress me ever so gently

They say love is blind but I disagree,
For If love was blind, it would never see
the way I connect with you and you with me

Love has a way of seeing way down deep in the soul,
Seeing things that no one else even knows

They say love is blind, but I disagree.

II

INTERMISSION:
LOVE DUETS

IN THE ROYAL KINGDOM...

Good morning My King, the sun has risen on our
Kingdom. May its rays brighten your day miles away.
Muuuaaahh!

Good morning my sweet love

I awake to wonderful thoughts of you

and therefore I am ready to start my day anew.

And most of all I Love You!

You are my queen, my sunshine

You are my everything that true love is

I love your every being

And no force can take that away

Being in love with you

Makes every morning

Worth getting up for

33

THE KING SPEAKS...

To the woman I love from the crown of her head

to the bottom of her feet

the sparkle in her eyes and her lips so sweet

I feel the same way and you can rest assure

my mind, body, & soul will be with you for eternity with

compassion and love

The sparkle in your beautiful brown eyes ignites the blood

that flows through my heart

and creates a spark that connects our souls to be as one

To a special friend that I've never forgot

A lot of time has passed as I look at my watch

Our relationship now has been kicked up a notch

She looks as good now as she did then

Even down to the softness of her skin

THE QUEEN SPEAKS...

You bring out the best in me

And then you propel me

To reach my destiny

You are so much a part of me

Because you are my heart you see

You are my angel without wings

You magnify life's simpler things

You are my jewel

You are my pearl

You are all I need in this world

It's twelve noon and I'm still in the bed

Got thoughts of you running all through my head

I'm feeling so sad and blue

because I can't hear from you

what is this sister supposed to do

I'm so in love with you

THE FRUIT OF THE LIPS...

Good morning my love

The apple of my eye

My sweetie pie!

Good morning my hear

And my sweet potato pie

You are truly my sunshine on a rainy day

Our love transcends eternity

I could never forget you

Not today, not ever

For you have entered my heart

Where you will remain forever

III

Rain

THE RAIN

Rain is cold, Rain is wet,

Rain saturates you with a feeling that you will never forget.

I close my eyes so I won't be distracted

from absorbing the cool freshness of every drop,

and so I won't be tempted to wish that it would stop.

I reach out my arms

So that I can freely feel what it has to offer.

Everything that the rain touches becomes so much softer;

For if it makes the flowers grow,

What harm can it be to me?

But rather teach me something that I need to know

And open my eyes to something I wouldn't ordinarily see.

I learn to embrace pain just like I embrace the rain

Rather than let it drive me insane

I allow myself to feel it as it flows off my heart

Because I know when it is over,

I have a fresh new start

MY HEART

If I give you my heart

will you tear it apart?

Or

will you love me forever

the way you have

loved me from the start?

LET THE WIND BLOW

When love doesn't live here anymore

Do I shut the door

Never to open it any more

nor allow my heart to soar?

Or do I open every window

And let the wind begin to blow

And allow my heart to freely flow?

WAIT AND SEE

Just because I say

I don't know where this relationship might go,

Doesn't mean I don't want you anymore.

Please don't walk out that door,

Wait, spend time with me some more.

You never know what's in store;

you don't know what can be

Till you wait and see.

There is more to me

than what the eyes can see.

Spend time with me,

talk to me,

Wine me, dine me; get to know me

Be patient with me.

Just wait and see…

WEATHER THE STORM

I am not a young girl anymore;
I don't get excited about short cheap thrills,
I want someone who is REAL.
Let me break it down and tell you the deal,
This is how I really feel...

Commitment and Longevity
Is what will carry me.
Not saying you immediately have to marry me,
But you better treat me much better than I treat me.

It's not what you do in the good times
That impresses me;
It's how well you weather the storms.

Will you still love me the same
When there is no sunshine, but only rain?

Can you stand by my side
When times get tough and rough?
Or will you hang up your hat
as if you've had enough?

43

WANT MORE

This is not how I want this relationship to be;

I want more than what you are giving me.

I feel like I am being cheated,

When more than anything

I just want to feel needed.

This passion is so very strong

But I want more…

I want to belong.

I want to be right in your comfortable arms

So big and strong.

Strong enough to hold me down

And loving enough to

Keep me around.

I want more…

PAIN

This is *So* Hard

I don't know what to do.

I'm *Really* missing you

And my heart is hurting too.

As soon as I awake, my heart begins to ache.

Now, all this seems like such a mistake.

I just can't seem to catch a break

From all this pain and misery.

Look what this heartache has done to me.

My joy has now turned to pain

And I feel like I am going insane.

Things have begun to change;

Nothing seems the same,

And yet I am still calling out your name,.

Even in all this pain

WHAT ARE WE GOING TO DO?

I can't believe I let myself love you again

Even when I knew the whole situation.

I just couldn't help myself;

I only knew how good it felt.

I feel so connected to you

Like you were made for me and I for you.

But now what are we going to do?

My love for you is so very true.

You need me and I need you,

But now what are we going to do?

REELIN' MY HEART BACK IN

I'm reelin my heart back in.

I can't believe I cast it out again

After you hurt me way back then.

But now I'm reelin it back in

Before it grows way too thin.

You are not ready for me now

Like you were not ready for me then.

If not now, I wonder when?

But it doesn't matter

'cause I'm reelin it back in.

I love you now just like I loved you then,

But for us it just doesn't seem to be workin'.

So I'm reelin my heart back in.

MEMORIES

I am packing up my memories.

I am putting them on the shelf.

The illusions, the fantasies, the fairy tales,

They have all gone and left.

I enjoyed them while they lasted,

But now I bid them all farewell.

Maybe I will write them down on paper

And maybe someday our story tell.

But, today

They take their place in history,

And why they left…

Will always be a mystery.

LOVE DON'T LIVE HERE ANYMORE

Love don't live here anymore

It moved when you walked out the door.

In the beginning you made

My heart soar far above the clouds

Beyond the horizon

Further than the mind could imagine.

The bond between us was so very strong,

So strong that no one could come between us

And nothing could do us any harm.

Nor could anything possibly go wrong.

Emotions were running so awesomely high

That fact I cannot deny.

The love we mad/e was so great

That one minute I'd scream your name

And the next I would break down and cry

Pure tears of pleasurable joy.

But now..

Love don't live here anymore;

It moved out when you walked out the door

SEE ME

You used to see me,
And
I used to see you.
We lost sight of each other somewhere along the way.
We can no longer see or hear each other.
Sad,
but oh so true.
Remember these words?
"Why you looking at me like that?"
Back then, we were looking;
Therefore we could see

I saw you
And
You saw me.
Somewhere down the line, we stopped looking;
Therefore we can no longer see
Or were those just illusions of you and me?

I choose to believe they were true
So that is what I will continue to hold on to
Even when I can no longer hold onto you.

AFFECTION

Affection is not all about loving and kissing,
Affection is as simple as you taking the time to listen;
Hold your own thought long enough to truly
Hear my heart.

No wonder I have been silent for so very long
Cause when I speak
You deem everything I say as wrong.

Yet, how can it be wrong
When it it's the words from my very own song?
On my heart is where they belong.

Because you have played such an intimate part,
I desire to share with you my whole heart.
But who are you to tell me
Where my feelings end and start?

You're missing out on a lot
When you don't hear my heart.
I once thought you really knew me

But that must have only been when
You were trying to woo me.

Come on baby, It's really not that hard.
My heart is just as soft as it can be.
You say communication is the key,
But that's a two way street
Where both of our hearts and thoughts
are supposed to meet.
So how can you arrive there without me?

Affection is what I seek,
Listening, that is intimacy.

LOVE SUICIDE

A love suicide doesn't happen overnight

There are warning signs here and there throughout the duration of the relation.

But there is so much imitation, emulation, and mutation that occurs along the way,

That somehow the object of admiration slowly fades away.

The joy, the excitement that once resounded so loud,

Has now disappeared into a cloud.

A cloud of despair, disappointment, and disdain;

For now someone is feeling that all the time, love, and energy has been in vain

That cloud of despair can drive one insane

Or it may disappear into thin air

And leave all those emotions hanging there;

There in the vapor, in the air.

Either way the person is no longer there.

Just their cloud of untapped feelings, love, & emotions remain.

53

Those clouds of love

Just hang

And hang